Who is Mike Pence?

let us demand that educators around America teach evolution not as fact but his theory that's Mike Pence the current vice president of the United States explaining evolution but he wasn't always like that Michael Richard pens was born in 1959 to a family of Catholic Democrats in Indiana pens himself was a Democrat for much of his youth he idolized JFK and voted for Jimmy Carter over Ronald Reagan because why would you elect the movie star he said at Hanover College Penn started hanging out with a different crowd he was drawn to one of his older fraternity brothers John Gable when he noticed a gold shiny cross hanging from Gables neck but it was the power of music that truly changed pence as he explained in a 2010 interview standing at a Christian music festival in a spirit Kentucky in the spring of 1978 I gave my life to Jesus Christ and that's changed everything I'm a Christian a conservative and a Republican in that order after a brief law career Penn's ran for Congress in Indiana against Democratic incumbent Bill sharp it was revealed that Penn set up his campaign as a for-profit corporation keeping some of the money for himself he lost two years later he ran against sharp again Pence's campaign set up a phony environmental advocacy group to call voters and tell them Sharpe was planning on turning the family farm into a nuclear waste dump Pence's campaign was caught he lost with 42% of the vote and swore off campaigning for a career in radio this is Mike Pence the Mike Penn show and other shows hosted by been aired locally for a decade thanks to all of you listening as a media personality pence also embraced the written word petting notable op-eds about how Millan is bad and cigarettes are awesome despite the hysteria from the political class and the media smoking doesn't kill he said it was around that time that pence would get back into his political career in 2000 he ran for Congress our campaign this year has committed itself to talking about Mike Pence and what Mike Pence believes I'm Mike Pence and I asked for your support to serve Indiana in Congress his campaign website flaunted a promise to give money to institutions which provide assistance to those seeking to change their sexual behavior a promise many read us a commitment to gay conversion therapy Penn's spokespeople denied that claim pence promised didn't gain much steam but he still used the seat in Congress to further his extreme beliefs his efforts focus on limiting women's access to health care blockading america's access to stem-cell research cutting Hurricane Katrina relief funds and changing the definition of rape twice want to urge my colleagues to stand with all of us to stand for life to stand for taxpayers let's end public funding of the largest abortion provider in America in 2012 he went on to run for governor of Indiana during his campaign he once again reportedly used campaign funds for personal needs he also accepted more than $200,000 from the Koch brothers he won during his governorship he implemented a law allowing discrimination against the LGBT community in the name of religion the law most notably came to a head when a pizzeria use it as justification to not cater gay weddings do you think it should be legal in the state of Indiana to discriminate against gays or lesbians George yes or no come on Hoosiers don't believe in discrimination and this is about protecting the religious liberty of every Hoosier of every faith and and we're gonna continue to work our hearts out to clarify that to the people of Indiana and the people of this great yes sir no should it be legal to discriminate against gays and lesbians it's worth noting that Penn's his own relationship is a little unconventional our only Stone reporter observed that Governor Pence referred to his wife Karen as mother pence also admits that he refuses to dine alone with women without his wife there which thereby limits the power of women who work with him but Pence's policies affected more than gay wedding pizza some argue that he worsened the effects of an HIV outbreak HIV rates were on the rise in a small rural county in Indiana linked to the sharing of drug needles governor Pence was made aware of the problem by the Centers for Disease Control but didn't act on it multiple people reported that he told him he had to wait and pray on it pence eventually allowed a needle exchange program but only after infections that skyrocketed I do not support needle exchange as anti-drug policy but this is a public health emergency and on the recommendation of the Centers for Disease Control I am authorizing a focused short-term limited needle exchange program if local officials deem that to be necessary and appropriate in the end more than 200 people were infected months later pens would be tapped as Donald Trump's vice president pen stayed mostly uninvolved with a scandal surrounding the campaign smiling and nodding through accusations of treason sexual abuse and corruption levied at Trump and team I think this is a good man who's been talking about the issues and that's all he has to do to remain one heartbeat away from the presidency and America is back

Vice President Mike Pence was tapped by President Trump in February of 2020 to take the charge on the United State's response to the growing coronavirus outbreak. Which has raised concerns considering he has a bad track record when it comes to managing the spread of infectious diseases. As of March 11, 2020, there have been at least 4,300 deaths globally from coranavirus, with 31 deaths reported in the U.S. alone. The United States has seemingly been unprepared to handle an outbreak of this scope, while the South Koreans have been able to use kits to test more than 90,000 of their citizens for coronavirus, the U.S. initially had trouble even manufacturing the kits. Meaning the scope of the spread of the virus in the U.S. is largely unknown. FDA commissioner Stephen Hahn said I'm happy to report that this weekend more than 15,000 testing kits have been released. Also, the FDA has approved a testing regimin that state and local officials can be using. There's no question more cases are on the horizon, and the guy tasked with leading the charge has a checkered past when it comes to epidemics. One study says Pence worsened the HIV crisis in Scott County, Indiana, by delaying action as a governor at the time. Here's Jose Antonio Vargas on the vice president. Let us demand that educators around America teach evolution—not as fact, but as theory. That's Mike Pence, the current Vice President of the United States, explaining evolution. But he wasn't always like that. Michael Richard Pence was born in 1959 to a family of Catholic Democrats in Indiana. Pence himself was a Democrat for much of his youth. He idolized JFK and voted for Jimmy Carter over Ronald Reagan because At Hanover College, Pence started hanging out with a different crowd. He was drawn to one of his older fraternity brothers, John Gable when he noticed a gold, shiny cross hanging from Gable's neck. But it was the power of music that truly changed Pence. As he explained in a 2010 interview, I'm a Christian, a conservative, and a Republican. In that order. After a brief law career, Pence ran for congress in Indiana against Democratic incumbent, Phil Sharp. It was revealed that Pence set up his campaign as a for profit cooperation— keeping some of the money for himself. He lost. Two years later, he ran against Sharp again. Pence's campaign set up a phony environmental advocacy group to call voters and tell them Sharp was planning on turning the family farm into a nuclear waste dump. Pence's campaign was caught. He lost with 42% of the vote and swore off campaigning. For a career in radio. This is Mike Pence. 'The Mike Pence Show' and other shows hosted by Pence aired locally for a decade. Thanks, to all of you listening. As a media personality, Pence also embraced the written word. Penning notable op-eds about how 'Mulan' is bad and cigarettes are awesome. It was around that time that Pence would get back into his political career. In 2000, he ran for congress. Our campaign this year has committed itself to talking about Mike Pence and what Mike Pence believes. I'm Mike Pence and I ask for your support to serve Indiana in congress. His campaign website flaunted a promise to give money to A promise many read as a commitment to gay conversion therapy. Pence's spokespeople denied that claim. Pence's promise didn't gain much steam, but he still used his seat in congress to further his extreme beliefs. His efforts focused on limiting women's access to health care, blockading America's access to stem cell research, cutting hurricane Katrina relief funds, and changing the definition of rape. Twice. I want to urge my colleagues to stand with all of us— to stand for life, to stand for taxpayers. Let's end public funding of the largest abortion provider in America. In 2012, he went on to run for governor of Indiana. During his campaign, he once again, reportedly used campaign funds for personal needs. He also accepted more than $200,000 from the Koch brothers. He won. During his governorship, he implemented a law allowing discrimination against the LGBT community in the name of religion. The law most notably came to a head when a pizzeria used it as justification to not cater gay weddings. Do you think it should be legal, in the state of Indiana, to discriminate against gays or lesbians? George— It's a yes or no question! Come on. Hoosiers don't believe in discrimination. This is about protecting the religious liberty of every hoosier, of every faith. And— and we're going to continue to work our hearts out. To clarify that, to the people of Indiana and the people of this great country— Yes or no, should it be legal to discriminate against gays and lesbians? It's worth noting that Pence's own relationship is a little unconventional. A Rolling Stone reporter observed that Governor Pence referred to his wife, Karen, as mother. Pence also admits that he refuses to dine alone with women without his wife there. Which thereby limits the power of women who work with him. But Pence's policies affected more than just gay wedding pizza. Some argue that he worsened the effects of an HIV outbreak. HIV rates were on the rise in a small, rural county in Indiana linked to the sharing of drug needles. Governor Pence was made aware of the problem by the Centers for Disease Control, but didn't act on it. Multiple people reported he that told them he had to Pence eventually allowed a needle exchange program, but only after infections had skyrocketed. I do not support needle exchange's anti-drug policy, but this is a public health emergency. And on the recommendation of the Centers for Disease Control, I am authorizing a focused, short-term limited needle exchange program—if local officials deem that to be necessary and appropriate. In the end, more than 200 people were infected. Months later, Pence would be tapped as Donald Trump's Vice President. Pence stayed mostly uninvolved with the scandals surrounding the campaign, smiling and nodding through accusations of treason, sexual abuse, and corruption levied at Trump and team. I think this is a good man who has been talking about the issues— And that's all he has to do to remain one heartbeat away from the presidency. America is back!

JUDY WOODRUFF: From the raid this weekend that ended with the death of the top leader of ISIS, to the planned withdrawal of U.S. troops from Syria, Vice President Mike Pence has been at the center of U.S. policy in the region. He and Secretary of State Mike Pompeo met over a week ago with Turkey's President Recep Tayyip Erdogan. And, afterward, they announced a temporary cease-fire in Syria. And then the vice president was next to President Trump, sitting, watching, as U.S. Special Forces tracked down al-Baghdadi. That raid is where we began when I sat down with Vice President Pence at the White House earlier today. We spoke before the House Democrats announced plans to vote on Thursday to formalize their impeachment inquiry. Mr. Vice President, thank you very much for talking with us. MIKE PENCE, Vice President of the United States: Good to see you, Judy. JUDY WOODRUFF: Let me start with the news this weekend. And there's been praise from all corners for the U.S. military, intelligence community, the president, since he announced this successful raid in Syria killing al-Baghdadi, the leader of ISIS. My question for you is, does this mean the threat from ISIS and the ideology it represents is now lessened? MIKE PENCE: Well, we believe it does. But let me begin by saying, as the world learned Sunday morning, this weekend was a great weekend for America. The most wanted man in the world, al-Baghdadi, is dead. And it's a tribute to the courage and professionalism of our Special Forces, the armed forces of the United States, our intelligence services. But let me also say, Judy, it's a tribute to the decisive leadership of our commander in chief, President Donald Trump. JUDY WOODRUFF: So, you say it's less of a threat, ISIS, and the ideology behind ISIS? Does that mean the decision to move the U.S. troops out of Northern Syria is now more justified? MIKE PENCE: Well, let me say first we -- we think the elimination of al-Baghdadi, the active leader of ISIS, will have a measurable impact on that terrorist organization. That being said, let me address your question specifically. The president has made it clear that, when our troops went into Syria, in combination with Syrian Democratic Forces, they went in for the purpose of defeating the ISIS caliphate. And they accomplished that in March of this year, with -- at great sacrifice of Syrian Kurds and great sacrifice of our forces, great professionalism and courage on both sides. The last inch of territory controlled by the ISIS caliphate was captured. And with the killing of al-Baghdadi, we believe that fight has gone on and will continue. But the president's decision to move forces out of the border region was -- in a very real sense, it was a reflection of the fact that our troops went into Syria to defeat the ISIS caliphate, but they had evolved into being troops simply patrolling the border between traditional Kurdish Syria and Turkey. And the president -- the president said we didn't need to be in that mission. He announced we were moving our troops out. Our troops are moving out. And now, because of that, we have achieved a cease-fire in the region. And we're calling on European countries to make that safe zone a reality. (CROSSTALK) JUDY WOODRUFF: Excuse me. Excuse me. Sorry to interrupt, but there's just a number of questions I want to ask you. But the reason I'm asking is because, as you know, what is being pointed out is the irony is this, that this raid was carried out successfully because American troops were there. And yet the president has decided to move them out. So, if the troops hadn't been there, could there have -- there couldn't have been a raid. The other point that's being made is that this raid was conducted with the help of America's Kurdish partners. The U.S. has decided to leave those Kurdish partners to the -- to the will of Turkey, who doesn't want them there. So, there's a lot to square that circle. MIKE PENCE: Well, first, let me take the issue with the suggestion that, if we no longer had Americans patrolling the border of Turkey in Syria, that we wouldn't have been able to accomplish this mission. We have troops elsewhere in Syria. We have troops in Iraq. All across the region, Judy, we have nearly 40,000 American forces deployed. The Special Forces, I can't say precisely where, but the Special Forces that deployed in the region would have been unaffected by the decision the president made to have troops come out of the border area. JUDY WOODRUFF: So, they weren't part of the -- they wouldn't have been part of this pullout? Is that what... MIKE PENCE: Well, I can't say where the troops deployed from. But what I can tell you is that the president's decision to remove troops from patrolling the border of Syria and the Turkish border had no impact on the capability, as we demonstrated this weekend, of moving this incredibly successful assault that brought the most wanted man in the world to justice. JUDY WOODRUFF: And yet what is being seen now is that, after that meeting that you and Secretary Pompeo had with President Erdogan, and agreed on a safe zone, not long after that, President Erdogan met with President Putin of Russia. They settled on a much larger safe zone. And the Turks went after the Kurds with will. Hundreds were killed. There's talk in the U.S. of war crimes being committed. So, my question is, was this truly a success, when the Turks got what they wanted in the first place? MIKE PENCE: President Trump sent our delegation to Turkey with one mission. And that was to save lives, to stop the military incursion by Turkey into Syria... JUDY WOODRUFF: But they... MIKE PENCE: .. and to bring a cease-fire to the section of the border that Turkish military were controlling at that time. JUDY WOODRUFF: But hundreds of Kurds were killed. MIKE PENCE: We -- there was fighting along the border. There's no question. And even after the temporary cease-fire took effect, there were some limited skirmishes. But, as General Mazloum told me, as he said after the temporary cease-fire became a permanent cease-fire, what President Trump was able to secure from Turkey was a commitment to allow our allies in the Syrian Democratic Forces to safely withdraw from that 20-mile area along the border. And reports are today that Syrian Democratic Forces are now in the process of withdrawing from a similar section along the Turkish border in Syria that is, frankly, controlled by Russian forces and by the forces of Syrian leader Assad. JUDY WOODRUFF: But did the Turks break the promise they had made to you to respect this safe zone, to go on and -- and create a much larger safe zone, which, in effect, shut the Kurds out of a much larger area than what you had originally negotiated on? MIKE PENCE: You know, I -- I -- our focus was to end the fighting in the area that Turkey's military was present. The discussions that they had with -- with Russia and with Syria itself about creating a buffer zone along the border is something that, frankly, has been talked about for years. It's -- this whole notion that we would essentially have a demilitarized zone that would be without Syrian Kurdish military forces, not Kurdish people, but Kurdish people live there now and will continue to, but also that, eventually, it would be without the military presence of Turkey in that area as well, that we would create a demilitarized zone. JUDY WOODRUFF: It just... MIKE PENCE: And we're in consultation right now, Judy, with our European allies to bring resources to bear and maybe well personnel to bear to -- to monitor that area. The only thing President Trump made clear was that U.S. forces would no longer be deployed along the border between traditional Kurdish Syria and Turkey. JUDY WOODRUFF: So, it's... MIKE PENCE: But the United States is fully prepared to work with and enlist the support, using our diplomatic and economic power, of other nations to maintain a safe zone. (CROSSTALK) JUDY WOODRUFF: Sorry to interrupt. So it's a success for Russia, who is celebrating this. Iran has come out ahead. And the Syrian regime has come out ahead. Just -- that's a victory for the United States? MIKE PENCE: No. No. When President Trump sent our team, he sent us with one mission, Judy. And that was to stop the invasion, to end the killing. And we accomplished that in a five-day cease-fire that literally allowed thousands of our allies in the Syrian Democratic Forces to safely withdraw from the area that was under control of the Turkish military. But make no mistake about it. To your point, President Trump has made it clear that American forces will remain in Syria, and particularly that we will be deploying forces to ensure the security of the oil fields all across Northern Syria. And we're going to be working very closely with our Syrian Kurdish allies to make sure that the revenues from those -- oil don't fall into Iran's hands, don't fall into the regime's hands, don't fall into Russia's hands, but they remain -- they remain focused on ensuring the security and the stability of those hard-fought gains, where our Syrian Democratic Forces literally won back their country from the scourge of ISIS. JUDY WOODRUFF: Let me turn to Ukraine and then the impeachment inquiry under way right now in Congress by the House of Representatives. The president, as you know, says he never pressured Ukraine's President Zelensky to investigate Joe Biden. But there's now reporting by a number of news organizations, including the Associated Press, that, as long ago as May, after the president's first phone call with President Zelensky, that he was strategizing, anxious, worried with his staff about how to deal with this pressure from President Trump. MIKE PENCE: Well, that's -- that's not what President Zelensky has said. He actually said there was no pressure. In his conversation with the president, he said... JUDY WOODRUFF: But the people around him... MIKE PENCE: ... that -- that, in discussions that I had with him, that there was no pressure. And I think any American who takes time to read the transcript of President Trump's call with President Zelensky will see the president did nothing wrong. There was no quid pro quo. JUDY WOODRUFF: But in that transcript, Mr. Vice President, the president mentions Joe Biden. And he says to President Zelensky, "I hope you will look into this," in a reference to what happened to Joe Biden's son, to Vice President Biden's son, and to Mr. Biden. What did you think when you read that in the transcript? Did you think that it was appropriate for the president of the United States to bring up a political rival? MIKE PENCE: Well, I think the president has made clear that his discussion in that matter was all about looking to the past. But -- and I can tell you that, in -- in the president's call, when the American people take time to actually read the call, which I know was greatly distorted by the way it was characterized... JUDY WOODRUFF: But what did you think... MIKE PENCE: ... in the whistle-blower's report. The whistle-blower spoke about eight different references to the Bidens. That was simply... JUDY WOODRUFF: But it's just the whistle-blower, Mr. Vice President. It... MIKE PENCE: And -- but the other thing, the other... JUDY WOODRUFF: It... MIKE PENCE: ... distortion, Judy, frankly, was when the chairman of the Intelligence Committee read into the record before the committee a fabricated version of the phone call. JUDY WOODRUFF: But it's not just... MIKE PENCE: That's why, any time this topic comes up, I always tell people, make sure and sit down and read the transcript, and you will see there was no quid pro quo. The president did nothing wrong. And I can assure people that, in all of my discussions with President Zelensky on the president's behalf, we were completely focused on restoring the territorial integrity of Ukraine, standing with them against Russian aggression, helping to support their efforts to deal with corruption in their country... JUDY WOODRUFF: But I -- excuse me. MIKE PENCE: .. and enlisting more European support. JUDY WOODRUFF: Excuse me for interrupting. But to bring up Joe Biden's name, the man who is likely to be, may well be the Democratic nominee for president next year, did it raise a red flag with you? And, by the way, it's not just the whistle-blower. It's William Taylor, longtime respected diplomat, appointed by President Bush, reappointed by President Trump, who said -- and I'm quoting -- based on everything he was told by people who talked to the president, that the president was withholding military aid for Ukraine and the promise of a White House meeting because they weren't committed to investigating the Bidens. This was in the transcript. You read that transcript. Do you -- does Bill Taylor, William Taylor, have credibility, as far as you're concerned? MIKE PENCE: Well, are you referring to William Taylor's testimony before the committee? JUDY WOODRUFF: His account, the testimony, as far as we know. MIKE PENCE: Well, I -- we can't really count on that, because all we have from the committee are leaks. JUDY WOODRUFF: Well, we have his statement. MIKE PENCE: I mean, Judy, the -- the process that's going on in Congress today is a disservice to the

American people, and it's a disgrace. I mean, to have impeachment hearings taking place behind closed doors, and the only thing the American people learn about are piecemeal release, leaked apparently by the Democratic leadership on the committee to the press. JUDY WOODRUFF: This was his opening statement, 15 pages. MIKE PENCE: It's just unacceptable, Judy. The -- the committee ought to release the entire record of all of their witnesses, how they responded, how they clarified points that they had made in their testimony. And the American people deserve to know that. I mean, the... JUDY WOODRUFF: Again, it wasn't leaked. It was in his statement that he released to the public. MIKE PENCE: Well, yes, according -- look, the American people have a right to know. Impeachment is a great and serious matter in the life of this nation, and the way the Democrats are conducting this so-called impeachment inquiry on Capitol Hill, behind closed doors, is wrong. And they should -- they should open this whole process to the light of day. They should release all of the transcripts. JUDY WOODRUFF: And they say they're going to do that, that they're moving toward an open process. MIKE PENCE: And they should also respect the due process rights of the president of the United States of America. JUDY WOODRUFF: And they say Republicans have an equal... MIKE PENCE: In the last two impeachment -- in the last two impeachment inquiries, you know, Judy, there were rules that were established where counsel could be in the room, where due process rights of the president and of the administration were respected. And that's simply not the case now. And I think it's why, as I travel around the country, it's why so many Americans are so frustrated with this Congress, because, frankly, for the last three years, Congress has been spending most of its energy trying to overturn the will of the American people in the last election. And despite the fact we have been able to get an enormous amount done, when we had a Republican majority in particular, and this weekend's extraordinary military success and the defeat and the killing of the most wanted man in the world in al-Baghdadi, shows that we're continuing in the fight to keep this nation secure. The S&P standard just set a record today. This economy is booming, 6.5 million jobs. And then the American people look at this Democrat Congress , and its endless investigations, and its so-called impeachment inquiry... JUDY WOODRUFF: I think Congress... MIKE PENCE: And I think the American people, Judy, are saying, enough is enough. They really want to see the Congress start to focus on issues that matter most to them, to their public safety, to prosperity. JUDY WOODRUFF: By the way, you mentioned previous impeachments. Lindsey Graham, who was in the House of Representatives during the Bill Clinton impeachment process, said at the time, the day Richard Nixon failed to answer the subpoena is the day that he was subject to impeachment, because he took the power from Congress, the point being that Congress does have a right to investigate a president. It says so in the Constitution. MIKE PENCE:

Well, Congress has this authority. And, so, the question is, why are... JUDY WOODRUFF: And they're asking the administration to cooperate. And... MIKE PENCE: No, remember, Judy, I was in the Congress for 12 years. The Congress acts by a vote in the majority. Even that hasn't happened here. The speaker of the House unilaterally initiated an impeachment inquiry. There's been no vote. Members of Congress have taken no position on this inquiry. And most members of Congress have no access at all to what's happening behind closed doors. I think the American people just deserve better. JUDY WOODRUFF: It's a process... MIKE PENCE: I mean, if Congress wants -- if Congress wants to pursue an impeachment, then they ought to do it in a way that respects the American people, gives the American people all the facts, and -- and ultimately respects the history and tradition of the House of Representatives, as well as the due process rights of the president. JUDY WOODRUFF: They say these three committees will wrap up their work in a couple of weeks, and then they will turn to open hearings. If the House goes ahead and votes to impeach the president, what do you believe will happen in the United States Senate? Do you believe they will convict the president and remove him from office? MIKE PENCE: Well, let's be clear first that I don't take it as a foregone conclusion that the House will -- will vote to impeach President Donald Trump. I mean, as the American people take a look at the facts in this case, they read the transcript, it was so mischaracterized by the whistle-blower, and grossly mischaracterized by Chairman Adam Schiff in his fabricated version of the phone call that he read into the committee. But when people read the transcript, they will see, despite the reckless allegations of many in the media, there was no quid pro quo. President Zelensky himself said there was no pressure, that it was a perfectly good phone call. The president did nothing wrong. And, as the facts all come out, I think the American people will come to understand that. And I expect they will let their voice be heard on Capitol Hill. But the other reason is -- is, I really think the American people really want to see this Congress come together and work with this president in ways that will make our country more secure and more prosperous. JUDY WOODRUFF: Mr. Vice President, thank you very much. MIKE PENCE: Thank you, Judy. Good to see you.

mike pence biography 1959 former u.s congressman and governor of indiana mike pence was elected vice president of the united states with president donald trump in 2016. who is mike pence u.s vice president mike pence was a conservative radio and tv talk show host in the 1990s after losing two bids for a u.s congressional seat he successfully ran for congress in 2000 rising to the powerful position of republican conference chairman before being elected governor of indiana in 2012. named donald trump's running mate in july 2016 pence became vice president of the united states when trump won the presidential race on november 8 2016 though their administration ended four years later with a loss to the joe biden kamala harris ticket eerie life family and education michael richard pence was born on june 7 1959 in columbus indiana one of six children of nancy and edward pence a u.s army veteran who operated a series of gas stations pence was politically influenced by the irish catholic leanings of his family he grew up idolizing former president john f kennedy and volunteered for the bartholomew county democratic party as a student at columbus north high school while church had played an important role in pence's early family life he became more deeply religious as a student at hanover college additionally although he voted for jimmy carter in 1980 he became inspired by ronald reagan and the republican party after graduating with a ba in history in 1981 he moved to indianapolis in 1983 to attend the indiana university mckinney school of law earning his jd in 1986. while church had played an important role in pence's early family life he became more deeply religious as a student at hanover college where he became a born-again evangelical catholic marriage and children pence has been married to wife karen since 1985. a former elementary school teacher karen has also been involved with youth-related nonprofit organizations the couple has three adult children michael charlotte and audrey early professional career pence went into private practice following his graduation and tried his hand at politics by becoming a precinct committee man for the marion county republican party seeking to make a bigger splash he ran for congress in 1988 and 1990 losing both times to democrat phil sharp however pence learned a valuable lesson in defeat disgusted by his own line of attack ads he penned an essay in 1991 titled confessions of a negative campaigner and vowed to preach a positive message from then on meanwhile his public profile continued to grow pence served as president of the indiana policy review foundation from 1991 through 1993 before making the leap to radio talk show punditry with the mike pence show referring to himself as rush limbaugh on decaf pence was unapologetic in his support of a conservative agenda but was commended for his level-headed manner and willingness to listen to opposing views his radio show was syndicated in 1994 and he branched out to television as a morning show host the following year before ending both programs in 1999 u.s congressman pence revived his political career by running for congress again in 2000 this time winning a seat describing himself as a christian a conservative and a republican in that order he quickly demonstrated that he wasn't afraid to buck party lines he opposed president george w bush's no child left behind policy in 2001 as well as the medicare prescription drug expansion the following year while his positions ranked party elders they bolstered his reputation as a man of strong convictions and he easily won re-election five times climbing the ranks of republican leadership pence was named head of the republican study committee in 2005. he was unsuccessful in his bid to become minority leader in 2006 losing to ohio's john boehner but two years later he was unanimously elected to the powerful position of republican conference chairman a staunch fiscal conservative pence insisted on cuts to the federal budget before supporting funding for hurricane katrina relief efforts in 2005 and was among the leading opponents of the federal bailout in 2008. he also drew attention for his social views notably supporting a plan to shut down the government over a fight to defund planned parenthood in 2011. indiana governor in 2011 pence announced his intention to run for governor of indiana the following year despite strong name recognition and the platform focused on tax cuts and job growth he became embroiled in a heated race with democrat john gregg eventually pulling out a close win with just under 50 percent of the vote after he became governor pence had his congressional papers which are housed at indiana university in bloomington sealed according to the donor agreement the public is forbidden from seeing his papers from the 12 years he served in congress until either december 5th 2022 or the death of the donor whichever is later in 2013 pence sealed the deal on a 1.1 billion dollars get back the largest tax cut in state history he also signed into law the state's first pre-k funding program and steered funds toward infrastructure improvements by 2016 indiana was enjoying a 2 billion budget surplus and a pristine aaa credit rating though critics pointed out that the state's wages were below national average pence found himself in the national spotlight and on shaky ground after signing the religious freedom restoration act in march 2015. intending to protect business owners who didn't want to participate in same-sex weddings pence instead encountered resistance from moderate members of his party and corporations that threatened to pull out of the state and he was forced to alter the bill to provide exemptions for lgbtq communities similarly he came under fire in the spring of 2016 for signing a bill to prohibit abortions when the fetus has a disability donald trump's running mate shortly after announcing his intention to run for a second term as governor pence returned to the national spotlight when he surfaced as the vice presidential candidate for likely 2016 republican nominee donald trump although pence had opposed some of trump's views he was believed to be a good running mate for the new york business mogul due to his ties to congressional leaders and strong support among conservatives pence had originally endorsed republican presidential candidate ted cruz during the primaries on july 15 2016 trump officially announced that pence was his choice for vice presidential nominee via twitter at a press conference a day later trump called pence a man of honor character and honesty if you look at one of the big reasons that i chose mike and one of the reasons is party unity i have to be honest trump said so many people have said party unity because i'm an outsider i don't want to be an outsider on july 20 2016 pence accepted his party's vice presidential nomination at the republican national convention in cleveland ohio he followed cruz who was booed off the stage for a speech in which he declined to endorse trump in his acceptance speech pence remained composed and spoke of his running mate trump you know he's a man known for a larger personality a colorful style and lots of charisma and so i guess he was just looking for some balance on the ticket donald trump gets it he's the genuine article he's a doer in a game usually reserved for talkers the vice presidential nominee continued and when donald trump does his talking he doesn't tiptoe around the thousand new rules of political correctness he's his own man distinctly american where else would an independent spirit like us find a following than in the land of the free in the home of the brave historic presidential election on november 8 2016 pence was elected vice president of the united states when donald trump won the presidential race defeating democratic candidate hillary clinton the stunning trump pence victory was considered a resounding rejection of establishment politics by blue-collar and working-class americans in the early hours of the morning after the race had been called in trump's favor pence spoke at the campaign's victory party at the hilton hotel in new york city this is a historic night this is a historic time pence said to the crowd of supporters the american people have spoken and the american people have elected their new champion on november 11 trump named pence to be the head of his transition team replacing new jersey governor chris christie pence's office also said he would continue to serve as indiana governor until his term ended on january 9 2017. back in his home state pence found himself in a legal battle to try to conceal the contents of an email sent to him by a political ally the email was connected with pence's decision to have indiana join other states in suing to block president barack obama's executive actions on immigration bill groth a democratic lawyer sought to have the contents of an attachment to the email made public in an appeal of an earlier court decision in which the indiana supreme court ruled that it was not for the court to decide whether to release the emails pence's defense team countered that the contents of the email were protected from being released under the state's access to public records act u.s vice president on january 20 2017 pence was sworn in on the steps in front of the u.s capitol by supreme court justice of the united states clarence thomas pence took the oath of office before donald j trump was sworn in as the 45th president of the united states a week after the inauguration the vice president spoke at the march for life anti-abortion rally in washington d.c be assured we will not grow weary pence told activists before the march we will not rest until we restore a culture of life for ourselves and our posterity vice president pence also highlighted the trump administration's support of the movement this administration will work with congress to end taxpayer funding of abortion and abortion providers he said and we will devote those resources to health care services for women across america in the first weeks of the trump administration pence defended the controversial rollout of president trump's executive order to ban immigrants from the predominantly muslim countries of iraq syria iran sudan libya somalia and yemen for at least 90 days temporarily suspend the entry of refugees for 120 days and bar syrian refugees indefinitely in an interview on fox news sunday the vice president said we are going to win the arguments because we're going to take the steps necessary to protect the country which the president of the united states has the authority to do president trump also put pence in charge of a commission to investigate alleged voter fraud in the presidential election the president who won the electoral college but lost the popular vote by nearly three million to clinton claimed that three to five million people had illegally voted in the election bipartisan politicians including paul ryan refuted the claim i've seen no evidence to that effect ryan told reporters i've made that very very clear at the very center of our democracy is the integrity of the vote the one person one vote principal pence said in an interview with fox news and it'll be my honor to lead that commission on behalf of the president and to look into that and give the american people the facts the vice president also played an important role in the confirmation of betsy devos president trump's nominee for education secretary amid protests from democratic critics and teachers unions that devos a billionaire charter school supporter with no public school experience was unqualified for the position the senate deadlocked in a 50 to 50 tie republican senators susan collins of maine and lisa murkowski of alaska joined their democratic colleagues in voting against devos on february 7 2017 vice president pence cast the historic tie-breaking vote to confirm her the first time a vice president has been called on to break a tie in a cabinet nomination michael flynn controversy a week later it was revealed that another trump appointee national security adviser michael flynn had misled vice president pence about his conversations with sergey kosliak the russian ambassador to the united states prior to the inauguration according to the washington post flynn privately discussed u.s sanctions against russia with that country's ambassador to the united states during the month before president trump took office contrary to public assertions by trump officials vice president pence had appeared on cbs news face the nation stating that flynn had told him that he and kosliak did not discuss anything having to do with the united states decision to expel diplomats or impose censure against russia flynn resigned on february 13 2017 after less than one month on the job and in his letter of resignation he wrote unfortunately because of the fast pace of events i inadvertently briefed the vice president-elect and others with incomplete information regarding my phone calls with the russian ambassador i have sincerely apologized to the president and the vice president and they have accepted my apology weeks later reports circulated that pence's personal website had been hacked due to the bizarre content being featured it turned out that viewers were confused by a parody site attributed to the vp created by funny or die branching out unlike president trump pence was said to have fostered strong relationships with the men who preceded him in the executive branch in november 2017 a news story revealed that pence conversed with obama's vp joe biden at least once per month and also met with bush's former second-in-command dick cheney their discussions were said to involve the exchange of ideas and advice with the former vps relaying valuable lessons learned during their administrations in late december pence made an unannounced trip to afghanistan to demonstrate american commitment to stability in the region more than 16 years after war broke out we've been on a long road together but president trump made it clear earlier this year that we are with you pence told afghan officials adding we are here to see this through in january 2018 weeks after president trump raised an outcry by announcing his recognition of jerusalem as israel's capital pence visited the region much of his trip focused on working with u.s partners to counter terrorism and helping christian minorities in the middle east though he also attempted to smooth over things with arab leaders that aspect didn't work out as well as pence and king abdullah ii of jordan publicly agreed to disagree over the decision to recognize jerusalem while palestinian president mahmoud abbas refused to even meet with the american vice president weeks later pence became a central figure in the politics surrounding the winter olympics held in pyeongchang south korea first his selection as head of the u.s delegation was criticized by openly gay men's figure skater adam rippon who cited pence's alleged animosity toward the lgbtq community ripon also reportedly rejected pence's overtures to meet though the vp's office denied having extended an invitation in february before the start of the games pence delivered a tough message to north korea with the announcement that more sanctions were forthcoming toward the end of the games the washington post reported that pence had planned to secretly meet with a high-level delegation of north korean leaders before they cancelled at the last minute the attempted meeting contrasted with the administration's public stance that there would be no dialogue until north korea first agreed to abandon its nuclear program returning stateside the vice president generated more controversy with his comments at a luncheon hosted by the anti-abortion organization susan b anthony list and life institute in late february i just know in my heart of hearts that this will be the generation that restores life in america he said adding if all of us do all we can we can once again in our time restore the sanctity of life to the center of american law space force in august 2018 pence delivered a speech at the pentagon in which he outlined the administration's plans to create a sixth branch of the u.s military the space force declaring we must have american dominance in space and so we will he noted that president trump would request 8 billion over the next five years to support military operations in that arena while such military expansion would require congressional approval the department of defense attempted to kick-start the process by identifying several steps to take in the meantime including establishing civilian oversight for the space force and creating a united states space command critics countered by calling it unnecessary expensive and likely to cause bureaucratic problems the following year pence was dragged into the house impeachment inquiry of president trump after the washington post reported that the vice president was involved in efforts to pressure ukraine into investigating 2020 presidential candidate joe biden around that time pence and u.s secretary of state mike pompeo traveled to ankara turkey where they successfully brokered an arrangement with president recep tayyip erdogan to allow the safe passage of kurdish forces from an area in northeastern syria under fire from a turkish military operation coronavirus response on february 26 2020 president trump announced that vice president pence would lead the administration's response to the coronavirus which originated in china and was spreading around the world citing his experience with the emergence of middle east respiratory syndrome mers as indiana governor pence stressed the importance of partnerships between state and local governments and health authorities when responding to infectious diseases and said he would determine the best options for action to see to the safety and well-being and health of the american people while his regularly scheduled press briefings were soon dominated by the presence of trump pence focused on delivering measured versions of the president's fluctuating pronouncements coordinating efforts with governors and addressing matters of supply shortages on monday march 9 he announced that testing capabilities had increased to the point where 5 million tests would be distributed by the end of the week with the administration looking to find ways to reopen businesses and schools by april the vice president raised eyebrows by visiting the mayo clinic in minnesota without a face mask late in the month saying he wanted to be able to look workers in the eye and thank them without being obstructed on october 2nd 2020 president trump revealed that he and wife melania had both tested positive for kovald19 pence and wife karen were also tested but the results came back negative 2020 vice presidential debate at the vice presidential debate on october 7 2020 pence faced tough questioning from moderator susan page in attacks from opponent kamala harris over the white house's response to the coronavirus pandemic that had already killed more than 210 000 americans the vice president defended the administration's efforts pointing to trump's early decision to suspend travel from china and promise that a vaccine would be ready in record time he also argued that the trump white house was better equipped to support americans at home and abroad over the environmental policies proposed by the biden harris team saying they will derail the economy 2020 election defeat although pence expressed confidence in a re-election victory the day's-long effort to count the ballots brought increasingly grim news for the incumbents until biden was declared as the president-elect on november 7 2020. while trump raged against the illegal voting and launched a flurry of lawsuits to challenge the results pence offered a more grounded perspective of the proceedings urging supporters to remain vigilant as the litigation played out on december 14 2020 all 538 electors in the electoral college cast their vote formalizing biden's victory over president trump in the 2020 presidential election biden received 306 votes and trump received 232. trump continued to insist that he won the election and he called on pence as president of the senate to reject the results of contested states when congress convened to formalize the electoral college vote on january 6 2021 however pence publicly broke with trump just before the start of the congressional meeting by issuing a letter which read it is my considered judgment that my oath to support and defend the constitution constrains me from claiming unilateral authority to determine which electoral vote should be counted and which should not that afternoon after the president held the rally in which he criticized his vice president and the weak republicans who refused to join his cause pence was among the lawmakers who were whisked to safety when an unruly mob broke into the capitol and clashed with police resulting in four deaths and the declaration of a public emergency by washington d.c mayor muriel bowser to those who wreaked havoc in our capital today you did not win the vice president said when order was restored and he went on to formally declare biden's victory just after 3 40 a.m on january 7.

Made in United States
North Haven, CT
05 December 2022

27957074R00028